Jedburgh Abbey

THE BORDERS
ABBEYS WAY

Mike Salter

FOLLY PUBLICATIONS

View looking east across Mertoun Bridge on the Tweed towards the Cheviots

ACKNOWLEDGEMENTS

The photographs are mostly by Mike Salter, who also drew the maps. Thanks to the staff at Aspect Design for their help in preparing illustrations and assembling artwork of the book for publication. Thanks also to Jean Cuddeford for proof-reading the book, and particular thanks to Charles Henderson, who made a special trip down to Selkirk from Auchtermuchy to take the pictures of the main square, Scott's statue, and Ettrick Mill.

DISCLAIMER

Every effort has been made to ensure information in this book is accurate and up-to-date, but the author/publisher does not accept any responsibility for any accidents to users, nor is any responsibility accepted for any problems that might arise through any of the information given being inaccurate, incomplete or out-of-date. Please take careful note of the suggestions about outdoor safety given on page 8.   A6091

AUTHOR'S NOTES

Distances are given in miles, still the most familiar unit of measurement for most British people. Although modern Ordnance Survey maps are metric, heights and amounts of climb in these walking guides are given in feet so as to avoid any ambiguity as to whether an m folowing a figure means miles or metres. The contours on the Landranger maps are at 10 metre intervals, i.e. crossing three of them means roughly 100 feet of climb.

ABOUT THE AUTHOR

Mike Salter is 54 and has been a professional author and publisher since 1988. He is particularly interested in the planning and layout of medieval buildings and has a huge collection of plans of castles and old churches he has measured during tours (mostly by bicycle and motorcycle) throughout all parts of the British Isles since 1968. Wolverhampton born and bred, Mike now lives in an old cottage beside the Malvern Hills. Since walking Land's End to John O'Groats in 2004 following his 50th birthday he has done many other long distance backpacking trails. He is a life member of both the YHA and English Heritage, and he is also a member of the Backpackers Club and the Mountain Bothies Association. His other interests include railways, board games, morris dancing and calling folk dances and playing percussion with an occasional ceilidh band.

Kelso Abbey

CONTENTS

Introduction to the Walk   4

Introduction to the Abbeys   6

Environmental Impact   8

Navigational Aids   8

Outdoor Safety   9

Route Description   10

Further Reading   24

Useful Websites and Other Information   24

INTRODUCTION TO THE WALK

The Borders Abbeys Way is a delightful 67m circular walk which has been developed between 1998 and 2005, mostly using existing footpaths and tracks. About 15 miles of the route is on level paths on riverbanks, so the walking is fairly easy and the route is well signposted with a symbol of a combined W and A usually in white. The circuit takes in the five towns of Melrose, Kelso, Jedburgh, Hawick and Selkirk, any one of which could be used as a starting point for a walk going round either clockwise or anti-clockwise. However, starting at Melrose for a clockwise circuit works well. It also allows a possible easier and shorter circuit of 51 miles around the four abbeys to Jedburgh and then using the St Cuthbert's Way to return to Melrose instead of walking the southern part of the circuit via Hawick and Selkirk, where the the walking is rougher, involves more climbs, and requires rather more care with navigation. Note that there is also a Four Abbeys cycle route using a different route and signed with cycle logos on blue fingerposts.

With five towns plus the villages of Newton St Boswells, Roxburgh and Denholm lying on the circuit, and the town of Galashiels lying just over a mile off it, there is no shortage of services such as shops and pubs. Each of the six towns offers a fair range of services, especially Hawick and Galashiels, which are considerably bigger than the others. The 14m between Dryburgh and Kelso is the longest section without services, and there is also a 12m section without services from Hawick to Selkirk. Public toilets are available in the five towns, at or near the staffed abbey ruins at Melrose, Dryburgh and Jedburgh, and also at Newton St Boswells. Water in the burns and rivers crossed by the path will have flowed over fields containing animals or crops likely to have been sprayed, and is unsuitable for drinking even if boiled.

With the closure in 1969 of the main line Waverley Route from Carlisle to Edinburgh and all the branch lines that joined it, the Borders was left entirely devoid of railways. From Berwick Melrose can be reached by buses bound for Galashiels. From Carlisle railway station a roughly hourly bus runs up via Hawick and Selkirk to Galashiels, from which there are frequent local buses to Melrose, and there are also many buses to and from Edinburgh. Other buses serve Jedburgh from Galashiels, and there are less frequent buses which connect Jedburgh with Kelso.

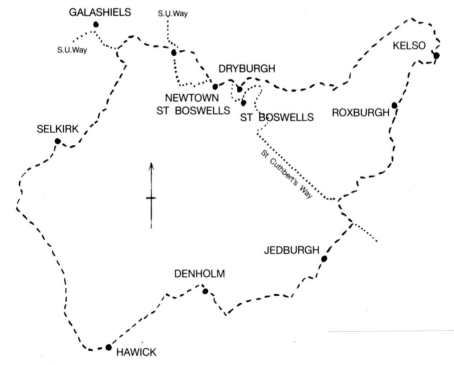

Wild deer on the path to the south of Jedburgh

Melrose has a youth hostel and there are plenty of hotels and B&B places in the towns and villages on and near the route. There are camp-sites at Melrose, Jedburgh and Selkirk. Wild camping is possible in some places but isn't encouraged either by the landowners or the authorities. Note that it is legal to stop for rest or refreshment when walking along rights-of-way but there is no right to erect any sort of shelter, however small or temporary. Some parts of the route will be unsuitable for wild camping because of animals or possible nocturnal fishing and shooting activities. If you do wild camp be discrete at all times, pitching out of sight of all roads and houses and leaving no trace that you've been there. Pitching late, leaving early, and using a tent with a flysheet of a colour that blends with the surroundings all help to make you invisible and thus less likely to be disturbed or moved on. Don't stay more than one night, camp in large groups, leave rubbish, light fires or make a lot of noise at any time of day.

Part of the ruins of Roxburgh Castle

INTRODUCTION TO THE ABBEYS

All four of the major abbeys along the Borders Abbeys Way were founded in the time of King David I, a period of great expansion in monasticism in Europe. An abbey he founded at Selkirk c1113 was moved to Kelso four years after he succeeded his brother Edgar on the Scottish throne in 1124. David founded the abbeys of Melrose and Jedburgh in the 1130s, and the abbey of Dryburgh was founded c1150 by the High Constable Hugh de Morville. The monks at Kelso were Tironensians following a reformed version of the Older of St Benedict. They fostered crafts and handiwork and thus attracted artisans. Melrose was the first of several Cistercian houses in Scotland. This order had lay-brethren to do the manual work in the fields and built churches with minimal ornamentation, high towers and other ostentatious features being forbidden. They aimed to be self-sufficient and built abbeys in remote places where sheep could be farmed. In contrast were the canons regular who were priests serving communities but living together in a monastic community. There were Augustinian canons dressed in black habits at Jedburgh, and the rather more austere Premonstratensian canons dressed in white habits at Dryburgh. All these monks and canons took vows of poverty, chastity and obedience. They were expected to attend up to seven church services during each 24 hour period, one of them being in the middle of the night.

It took many years to construct all the buildings of an abbey in stone, so many of the buildings would have been timber framed to start with. Changes to the intended plan, alterations, major repairs and additions were common, so that abbeys usually ended up as a hotch-potch of structures designed in different styles from various periods. All the abbeys, like all other buildings, suffered damage as a result of the wars between England and Scotland, partricularly in the early and late 14th centuries and during the first half of the 16th century. By that time some of the abbeys had lay rulers known as commendators rather than abbots. The monastic communities were dispersed during the Reformation in Scotland of 1559-60. At Melrose and Jedburgh parts of the churches were adapted for parochial worship and remained in such use until the 19th century, whilst at Dryburgh the church was largely dismantled for its materials but parts of the cloistral buildings remained in use. Historic Scotland now maintains the ruins of all four abbeys.

Dryburgh Abbey

Jedburgh Abbey, doorway between church and cloister

By the 12th century abbeys tended to be laid out on a common plan, but with minor variations to suit the particular needs of each order. Churches were usually cruciform with an aisled nave to the west of a central tower, the monks choir and presbytery containing the high altar to the east, and transepts on either side with semi-circular apses or square chapels containing altars projecting from their eastern walls. The extra western crossing with a second tower at Kelso was very unusual. The naves of abbey churches were often open to lay parishoners, except in the case of the Cistercians, where the monks choir usually lay under the central crossing, and the lay-brethren had their own choir stalls in the nave, a separate chapel near the gateway of the monastic precinct being provided for layfolk. The other main monastic buildings were usually placed on the south side of the church so that the cloister walks linking these rooms would catch the sun. The west range was used to accommodate lay-brethren in Cistercian monasteries, but in houses of other orders might contain cellarage and accommodation for the abbot and lay guests. The south range usually contained a refectory in which the monks or canons ate in silence whilst one of their number read gospels to them from a pulpit. In Cistercian houses the refectory was placed at right-angles to the cloister, which usually allowed space for a kitchen alongside. The upper storey of the east range formed the dormitory. At the north end steps led directly down into the church for easy access for night-time services. At the south end was the latrine or reredorter. The drainage that was required by latrines and kitchens occasionally resulted in the placing of the cloistral buildings on the more shaded north side of the church, as at Melrose. Below the dormitory lay a sacristy or vestry, a passageway out to the cemetery further east, rooms used for the training of novices, and a warming room, the only place where monks could ever gather and talk in front of a fireplace. A room called the chapter house, in which the monks gathered daily to conduct business and hear read a chapter of the rules of the order to which they belonged, also lay either within the lower storey of the eastern range, or projected from it, with access by a passage through the range. There would normally be several other buildings away from the cloister, for instance for an infirmary, or for an abbot's house or kitchen or bakehouse. There would also be the usual ranges of barns and workshops required by any large farm, although these might be timber-framed.

ENVIRONMENTAL IMPACT

Basically: Leave nothing but footprints, take nothing but photographs & memories. So:
Don't leave any litter, even biodegradable material such as fruit cores and skins.
Don't pick flowers or damage trees and plants, except where necessary to clear a path.
Don't make a lot of unecessary noise, especially when near houses or farm-steadings.
Don't get so close to any animals that they become stressed and abandon their young.
Don't stray from the path on sections where you can clearly see its intended route.
Don't touch farming or forestry equipment, crops, timber stacks or building materials.
Leave all gates as you find them, whether open or closed.
Be discreet if wild camping (see page 5), and guard against all risk of starting fires.
Use public transport to reach and leave the path if at all possible.

Use public toilets where possible. If you have to go outdoors make sure you are at least 30m from running water and try to bury excrement in a small hole where it will decompose quicker. Do not bury tampons or sanitary towels. You will have to carry these out. Ideally you should also do this with toilet paper also, since it doesn't decompose quickly and will blow around if dug up by animals.

If you are taking a dog with you it will need to be on a short lead at all times since there will be sheep or cows in some of the fields, and there are also some sections on roads. Also you will need to think carefully about where you will be able to stay.

NAVIGATIONAL AIDS

The route described in this book crosses the Ordnance Survey Landranger maps numbered 73, 74, 79 and 80. A compass could be useful, although there aren't much in the way of remote moorland sections. Although not essential, a useful item is a Global Positioning System. You can check your speed and distance, and time travelled, but best of all it will give you a grid reference accurate to a few feet. Those who like treasure hunting can additionally use the unit to find geocaches (website details given on page 24), of which there are a few on and near the route. GPS units use up batteries quickly, and need a clear view of the sky, so they are not so good in thick woods.

The southern parts of the buildings around the cloister at Jedburgh Abbey

Melrose Abbey

OUTDOOR SAFETY

Make sure you are wearing footwear suitable for the nature of the terrain. Boots or trail shoes are essential for the southern half of the circuit, where there are more climbs and sections of path through fields of potentially long wet grass. Sort out any problems with feet, footwear or socks immediately. Make sure you carry enough dry clothes to remain warm even in the most wet and stormy conditions, and carry enough food and drink so that you don't have to rush unduly or take risks. Be realistic when estimating distances. Don't expect to make more than three miles an hour even if fit, lightly loaded and weather conditions are favourable.

Kelso Abbey

ROUTE DESCRIPTION

MELROSE

Although it did a fair trade in linen in the early 18th century, Melrose has never been much of a manufacturing town, and in the last two hundred years has been largely a tourist centre, to some degree dependent on its abbey as it was during the medieval period. Recreational fishing opportunities provided by the River Tweed were stimulated by the arrival of the railway (now closed) in 1849. The station building now forms offices and a restaurant. The town offers plenty of accommodation, several shops and a tourist office opposite the abbey, with toilets nearby. Apart from the abbey the only ancient structures of note are the Market Cross dated 1645 with initials of John, Earl of Haddington, and a much-altered bridge of 1762 over the Tweed. The parish church has a tower of 1808-10 which survived the fire of 1908.

The original monastic settlement in this district, of which St Cuthbert was once a member, lay in a loop of the Tweed at Old Melrose nearly three miles further east. The present abbey was founded by David I in 1136 and colonised with monks from the Cistercian abbey of Rievaulx in Yorkshire. The church was rebuilt immediately after being destroyed by Richard II of England during his invasion of 1385 and has fine late medieval tracery in the windows of the east end and the south transept. Despite the collapse of the eastern part of the central tower (which probably carried a spire) and the adjoining eastern arches, this remains one of the finest medieval buildings in Scotland, and some parts still remain of the high vaults built in the 1450s and 60s. In the church was buried the heart of Robert I (the Bruce), who amassed funds for repairs after an English attack in 1322. The nave has an outer line of extra chapels beyond the south aisle. The eastern part of the nave formed the monks' choir and was later adaped as a parish church, piers being inserted on the north side in the 1620s to carry a pointed barrel-vault which still survives. The western part of the nave was never completed. North of it lies the site of the cloister. A 12th century sacristy adjoining the north transept remains complete with its vault, but only footings remain of the other buildings. These parts were uncovered by excavations in the 1920s and 30s after the ruins were taken into state care. The northern parts of the ranges are obscured by a road, beyond which stands the Commendator's House, now a museum with the date 1590 and initials of James Douglas over the entrance, and footings of the Abbot's House. Hardly anything remains of the refectory in the north range and not much of the 13th century chapter house projecting from the east range, but there is rather more of the lay brothers' part of the abbey in the west range.

Aerial view of Melrose Abbey

The Commendator's House at Melrose

Temple of the Muses at Dryburgh

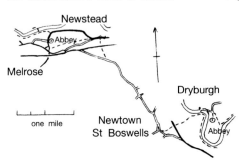

The Orchard Gate at Dryburgh

From the abbey entrance go south down Abbey Street back towards the Market Cross and turn left down Priorswalk, a path at a corner of the railings of the abbey grounds. Go left after a footbridge to reach a housing estate. Head straight on and then turn along a narrow path in front of a row of houses. This leads through to the village of Newstead, 1m from Melrose. Here lived the masons that built the abbey, and a lodge of masons was based here in St John's Wynd until it transferred to Melrose in 1741. East of the village lay the Roman fort of Trimontium, commemorated in monuments erected in 1928 and 2000. After going only a short section along the main street of the village turn right to go under the old railway line and the new bypass. The track climbs the NE flank of the Eildon Hills to reach what was once a main road, now closed to through traffic. Turn left and pass the stone marking the reputed site of the Eildon Tree where Thomas the Rhymer delivered his prophesies in the second half of the 13th century. Follow the road down into Newtown St Boswells, 3m from Melrose.

Turn right onto a road through the village and pass toilets in front of the building of the Scottish Borders Council. Turn left into Tweedside Road by the Bank of Scotland and after 100yards go left between buildings to join St Cuthbert's Way as it takes a track, later a path, down into Newtown Glen, which is a designated site of special scientific interest on account of the fauna and flora found here. The path climbs and follows the bank of the Tweed, finally dropping steeply to meet a road. Cross the river by going over the 260ft long suspension bridge dating from 1817, the first chain bridge built in Britain, and turn right. To the left above the corner here is a rock bearing a Temple of the Muses, a neo-Grecian pavilion also of 1817, built by the 11th Earl of Buchan and dedicated to the poet James Thomson. The original statue of the Apollo Belvedere has gone missing and been replaced in 2002 by bronze figures of the Four Seasons by Siobhan O'Hehir. The road to Dryburgh Abbey, which is 4m from Melrose, passes the Orchard Gate, a sandstone arch of c1820 forming the main entrance to Orchard Field, whilst to the west of the abbey is a 19th century house converted into an hotel in the 1930s

The Chapter House entrance at Dryburgh Abbey

Dryburgh has the most beautiful location of the four abbeys, being set within a wide, wooded loop of the Tweed. It is the burial place of the writer Sir Walter Scott, who died in 1832, and was colonised in 1152 by Premonstratensian canons from Alnwick in Northumberland. The abbey was burned by English armies under Edward II and Richard II in 1322 and 1385, and it was again devastated by fire in 1461. Considerable damage was again done by English invaders in 1544 and 1545. Of the church there remain only the west front, the outer wall of the south aisle containing a fine doorway through to the cloister, parts of the transepts with the side chapels still retaining vaults on the north side, and the lower parts of the presbytery. The western range and the detached gatehouse closeby to the SW of the cloister are unusually modest, and apart from one high gable not much remains of the south range which contained the refectory, but there are substantial remains of the late 12th century east range, including the well-preserved chapter house with its vault and ornate entrance. Between the chapter house and the south transept of the church with its well-preserved gable lie the parlour and sacristy, and further south were the warming room and novices day room, whilst the upper storey contained the canons' dormitory. SE of the abbey lies Dryburgh Abbey House, much of which post-dates a fire in 1892. A tower house built here by George Haliburton of Mertoun in 1572 was demolished by David Erskine, 11th Earl of Buchan, who landscaped and tidied up the abbey ruins, in which he was buried in 1828.

After leaving the abbey pass right of the toilets on a track for 150yards and then go left onto a path beside the Tweed. The path climbs up through trees, gives views of New Mertoun Bridge dating from 1839-4, and turns sharp left. Go right onto a road beside Mertoun cemetery. The road bends as it passes Clintmains and drops down to the B6404 directly opposite the entrance to Mertoun House, the gardens of which are open to the public during summer weekends. The church of 1658 was built by the Mein family of masons based at Newstead, and the house was begun in 1703 to a design by Sir William Bruce for Sir William Scott of Harden. There is also an older house of the 1670s in the walled garden, an ice-house, and a dovecot dated 1576 on the entrance doorway.

Turn right to follow the B6404 eastwards away from the river. After 300 yards a path in adjacent woods gets you off the road for a similar distance up to a right hand turn down a road past the farm steading of Magdalenehall. The road becomes a track down to the bank of the Tweed, which is followed for a mile, passing a fishermen's hut. Just before the hut the ruin of 16th century Littledean Tower lies above the other side of the river but is usually obscured by trees. Just after the track leaves the river go right through a gate and climb up past Old Dalcove, which lies on the site of a tower house destroyed by the Earl of Hertford in 1545. Pass through a gate onto a track. On reaching a corner of a road turn right, looking left to see the 16th century tower of the Pringle family on a high rock 2m to the NW at Smailholm. When the road ends at Dalcove Mains turn right down a track and follow it round to the left to reach Makerstoun, nearly 11m from Melrose. Turn left and then right just before reaching the church dating from 1808. After half a mile go left and immediately right to pass Haymount. Cross over the B6397 and pass Wester Muirdean on a leafy track.

Cross over the A6089, using a verge beside a lane to pass Harrietfield. After another 200 yards go right onto a track which drops to a burn and then climbs to the B6364. Go left a short distance and then find a stile on the right and follow the field edge round. Go through a gate and shortly after turn left onto a green lane. Turn right onto a road and pass Berryhill to turn right and pass along the western edge of Kelso Racecourse, which opened in 1822, and has a grandstand of that date. Turn left, follow the road round to the right and then turn left onto another road. Just before a petrol station on the left go right on a tarmac path between the houses. Zig-zag down a hill and turn right. Go through to another road and turn left along the A6089 for a short distance until there is access on the right to the Cobby Riverside Walk along the north bank of the River Tweed. At the end of this an alley leads through to Roxburgh Street. Go left to find a supermarket, otherwise go right to enter the main square of Kelso, where there are many other shops. Pass down the right (SW) side of the square onto Bridge Street to reach the abbey ruins, 18m from Melrose.

Bridge over the River Tweed at Kelso

In 1128 David transferred a Tironensian abbey founded at Selkirk fifteen years earlier to a site here at Kelso, where it was closer to the royal castle and town of Roxburgh. The abbey was wrecked by the English in 1545 and then dismantled for its materials. Part of the abbey church remained in use until an octagonal new parish church was built in Abbey Row in the 1770s, and at one time there was a vaulted prison in the roof of the building. All that now remains of the church are the impressive western pair of transepts and the south and west walls of the tower between them, plus part of a lofty western porch or vestibule and two bays of the arcade between the nave and the south aisle. A parlour adjoins the southern transept. Excavations have revealed one of the piers which supported the main central tower further east and footings of a building some way to the SE which was thought to be the infirmary. There are no remains of the other buildings.

At first the town was just a small village outside the abbey gates and it only grew into a town in the 15th century after the decline of the town of Roxburgh on the other side of the Tweed (see page 15). Kelso later became a centre for making coaches, agricultural machinery, furniture, and fishing tackle, but the dukes of Roxburghe residing in Floors Castle 1m to the west prevented the town from becoming too industrial and the population peaked just under the 5000 mark in the 1850s, despite a railway arriving in 1851. The large main square has mostly late 18th century buildings. A tourist office lies within the town hall of 1816. Floors Castle was built by John Ker, first Duke of Roxburghe in the 1720s to replace an older tower house. It was remodelled in 1837-47 for the sixth Duke and is open to the public in the summer months. The estate includes a long length of riverside path and it is unfortunate that the Borders Abbeys Way does not use it.

Kelso Abbey

Wallace's Tower near the village of Roxburgh

From Kelso Abbey continue down Bridge Street and cross over the bridge of 1801-4. On either side of the town end of the bridge are an original toll-house and a pillbox of the 1940s. Opposite where you turn left on the A699 is an archway designed by James Gillespie Graham in 1822 which formed the main entrance to Springfield Park House, a mansion of the 1750s and 1820s demolished in the 1950s. Follow the main road as it bends left opposite the confluence of the Tweed and Teviot and cross over the Teviot on a bridge of 1795. After 250 yards there is access to a path on the west bank of the Teviot. This passes below the overgrown ruins of Roxburgh Castle perched on a large natural mound 85ft high between the two rivers (see page 5). It was a royal castle, first mentioned in 1128, and one of Scotland's largest and greatest strongholds ranking alongside those of Berwick, Edinburgh and Stirling. For much of its history the castle was in English hands, being rebuilt by the English kings Edward III, Richard II and Henry V, with the Scots frequently trying to get it back. Here in 1460 James II of Scotland was killed during one such siege when one of his own cannon blew up alongside him. His queen had the castle stormed and destroyed. The remains were incorporated into an English fort at the end of Henry VIII's reign in the 1540s, but this was dismantled when Edward VI withdrew his troops from Scotland in 1551 under the terms of the Treaty of Bologne. The castle protected the only access to the town of Roxburgh between the confluence of the Tweed and Teviot. Nothing remains visible of this town, although it once had walls and gates, two churches, schools, many houses and shops, and a Franciscan friary.

Passing an open shelter two thirds of a mile SW of the castle, the path continues along the river bank to Roxburgh Mill Farm and then a road leads into the village of Roxburgh, a settlement by a former junction station two and half miles from the original medieval town. Go left down a lane past a furniture workshop to regain the river bank and then go under the railway viaduct. Alternatively go a bit further through the village and in the bus-stop next to where the railway once crossed the road are boards with much history of the village, especially the story of how two arches of the railway viaduct collapsed through failure of a pier during construction work in 1847. Access over the river to the village of Heiton, a set of five caves on the east bank of the river, and the Roxburghe Hotel and golf course is possible by means of a footbridge suspended from the viaduct. The path between the bus-stop and the river-side path just north of the viaduct gives a view of a late 16th century ruin called Wallace's Tower in an adjacent field. It belonged to the Kerr family and is mostly destroyed above the vaulted cellars.

Railway viaduct at Roxburgh

Beyond the railway viaduct continue on the river bank for a mile before turning right opposite a small island. Follow the field edge up to a stile and steps to turn left onto the trackbed of a railway. After half a mile a missing bridge necessitates going down steps to a road, going left and then immediately right to get back on the railway line for another two and a half miles to Nisbet, which lies 26m from Melrose, and 8m from Kelso. On reaching the B6400 turn left, away from the village, to cross over the Teviot, and then use the path on the floodbank to pass the next bend of the river. Go left to a track, then right to gain a track upon a further section of old railway trackbed. This leads round to join the A698. Go right and then cross the road to go left up a lane, before forking left on a track climbing the hill on the line of the old Roman road of Dere Street which once linked York with Edinburgh. After half a mile St Cuthbert's Way continues up a short distance more before turning left, whilst the Borders Abbeys Way goes right onto a green lane. It descends to a road after a mile. Go left and cross over another road to reach a footbridge over the Jed Water. Go left down the A68 a short distance to take a path on the west bank of the Jed Water. Cross the river below cliffs, keep on the east bank, and then recross the river to go up Bridge Street and then into the High Street of Jedburgh, 31m from Melrose and 13m from Kelso.

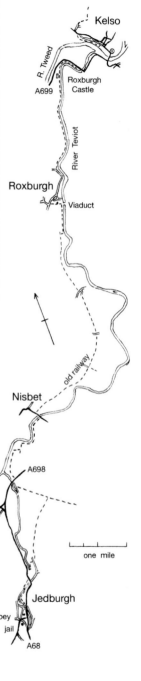

Jedburgh Abbey

Jedburgh existed in the 830s, part of a shrine or screen of that period remaining amongst the carved stones in the new visitor centre of the abbey. Certainly there was a church and royal castle before David I founded the abbey for Augustinian regular canons c1138. A castellated jail of the 1820s, open to the public and of considerable interest, lies on the site of the once-important castle on a knoll at the far south end of the town. The castle had two towers and was destroyed in 1409 to prevent the English occupying it. The jail is a reminder that Jedburgh was once the county town of Roxburghshire, taking over this function after the decline of Roxburgh. The town had several mills for grinding flour and meal, and malting and distilling were once important. The wool trade was stimulated by the arrival in 1856 of the railway along the trackbed you have already walked. A rayon factory which opened in 1929 and closed in 1956 led to a doubling of the population of the town. A road named The Friars was the only reminder of the former Franciscan Friary until excavations between 1983 and 1992 revealed footings of parts of the church, cloister and buildings, now displayed in a public garden. Several towers lay in the town when it was devastated by the English in the 1540s. A house in Queen Street is named after Queen Mary, who stayed in Jedburgh for a month in 1566, although it may actually be at least a generation later than that. Now a museum, it is a T-plan building with a a staircase wing on the east side and a hall and chamber over a vaulted passage, cellar and kitchen. The market place in the centre of the town was opened up by removing the tolbooth or town hall in 1759, whilst the mercat cross was taken away in 1866.

The abbey ruins lie on a series of terraces descending southwards from the church down to the Jed Water. Substantial undercrofts, once vaulted, remain of southern ranges containing the refectory, the abbot's house, and the reredorter or latrine at the south end of the dormitory in the east range, but only footings remain of the cloister and most of the west and east ranges. Much of the 12th and 13th century church stands almost complete, including the central tower, but the loss of the ends of both the south transept and presbytery give the ruin a slightly odd appearence. The south transept had an east apse and was truncated by a cut-off wall as early as the 16th century. The north transept lost its east apse when it was rebuilt and extended in the mid 15th century. In 1681 it was divided off by a wall to enclose a burial aisle for the Kerr family. Arcades of nine arches dating from c1180-1220 divide the nave from its aisles, and the choir is flanked by chapels two bays long. A new church was formed in the western half of the nave and north aisle in 1668-71, but all evidence of this was removed in 1875, when a new parish church was built elsewhere in the town.

Cliffs above the Jed Water at Jedburgh

Queen Mary's House at Jedburgh

Outer wall of the old jail on the castle site at Jedburgh

From Jedburgh abbey return to the Square and climb up Castlegate to go left of the jail. The road becomes a track and then a footbridge is crossed to reach another track passing Todlaw. At a T-junction turn right up a hill and go left at a junction of tracks along the old road from Jedburgh towards Swinnie. Go over several stiles and drop down right (not currently signed) onto a footbridge to climb up beside the plantation of Merlin Dean. Go through a gate to reach a path through the top end of the plantation to another gate. Turn right and follow the waymarkers over the shoulder of Black Law, about 1000ft above sea level. There are radio masts on the summit of the hill to your right. Cross a stile to go down the right hand side of the wood known as Blacklaw Strip. At the far end go left and cross a burn and a stile onto a track. Turn right at the second gate and head down the farm track to a road. The way goes left here but turn right to visit the church of Bedrule which lies 35m from Melrose via Kelso and Jedburgh. The church is now mostly a rebuilding of 1914 of a structure of 1804 and 1877. In the porch under the tower are a small medieval relief effigy with a sword and two fragments of 11th and 12th century hogback stones with tegulated decoration. Above a loop of the Rule Water not far to the NW are scanty overgrown traces of a 13th century stone castle of the Comyns. It had a large court with several circular flanking towers and a gatehouse facing NW.

After returning to the junction near the church and passing the war memorial turn right to cross over Rule Water on a mid 19th century bridge. Shortly after swinging right take a left turn onto a road for 400 yards, climbing steeply. When the road goes left take the track going straight on to a plantation. The track goes left and a stile is then crossed into a field. Turn right and follow the fence to cross a stile beside a gate. Go straight on along the field edge, eventually turning left to follow a wall to a gate. Cross a field and a ladder-stile and a burn to join the track to the farm of Spital Tower. When the track goes right the way goes left over a stile and follows the fence to another stile. Go left over a small bridge and go up the left side of the fields. Go left alongside the wood and then find a gate on the right leading through it. A stile then gives access onto the top of a green lane known as The Loaning which leads down into the A698 leading into Denholm, which lies 38m from Melrose via Kelso and Jedburgh. The village was laid out in the late 18th and early 19th century around a green, in the centre of which is a monument to the poet, physician and antiquarian Dr John Leyden, 1775 -1811, a native of Denholm. The village was once noted for stocking weaving and has a shop, post office and pub.

The village green at Denholm

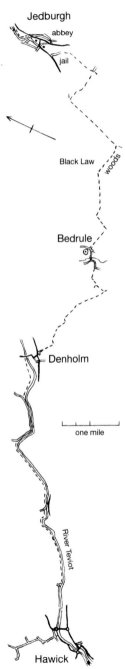

Jedburgh
abbey
jail
Black Law
woods
Bedrule
Denholm
one mile
River Teviot
Hawick

Turn right off the A698 to pass along the northern edge of the green at Denholm. Follow the road round to the right and left and cross over the Teviot on the three-arched bridge of 1864. Turn left to drop onto the path along the north bank of the river, keeping to the floodbank to reach a track. Return to the floodbank, cross two stiles, go up steps to follow the edge of a field and then drop down to turn left onto a road beside the river. After about a mile a path goes left to remain on the river bank when the road climbs away from it. The path then follows the river bank and passes the Teviotdale Leisure Centre (containing pub lic toilets) before joining roads along the riverbank for the final mile to meet the A7 into Hawick, which lies 44m from Melrose via Kelso and 13m from Jedburgh.

With a population of about 16,000 Hawick is the largest town in the Borders, having expanded in the late 18th and early 19th centuries as a centre for textiles and woollens with many water and steam powered mills. A railway arrived from Edinburgh in 1849, and was continued through to Carlisle in 1862. The town is now centred on the High Street, in which lies the Horse Monument, a bronze mounted standard bearer of 1921 which commemorates the capture of an English flag by Hawick youths in 1514, an event with cheered the Scots after the recent disaster of James IV's defeat and death at Flodden. The monument is the focal point of the Common Riding ceremonies. The tourist office lies at the south end of the High Street, in a later wing adjoining the tower of the Douglases of Drum-lanrig built c1570 by the former old bridge over the Slitrig Water. The tower later passed to the Scotts of Buccleugh and in 1769 became an inn, continuing in that role (as the Tower Hotel) until shortly before it was restored in the 1990s. Go over the later bridge over the Slitrig (originally of 1770, but much widened in 1828 and 1900) and take the second left (Howgate) to pass some toilets and reach the original medieval town centre between St Mary's Church and the 12th century motte of the earth and timber castle of the Lovel family 400 yards south of the bridge. Amongst the buildings here burned in the English attack of 1548 were three tower houses. The church has a transept and other parts of 1764 and was much rebuilt and altered in 1882-3 after a fire, but parts of the main body may have portions of medieval walling.

The motte at Hawick

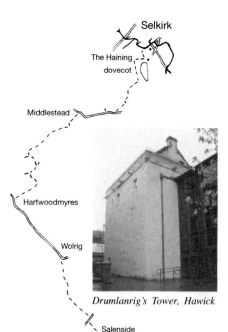

The Horse Monument at Hawick

Drumlanrig's Tower, Hawick

From the centre of Hawick go back along the High Street and cross over the Teviot beside the A7. Turn left into Princes Street for 200 yards and then turn right up Dickson Street to pass Wilton Parish Church, a building of 1860. Note the unusual spiralled brick chimneys on the adjacent church hall. SE of here a few memorials in parkland mark the site of a former medieval church, since Wilton was a village in its own right before becoming a suburb of Hawick. The road continues to climb as it bends right then left, and passes (all on the right-hand side) a school, a road, and St Andrew's convent. After a steep climb up from a crossing of a burn go over a crossroads known locally as the Fower Roadends. Beyond the tracks going left to Tandlaw and Drinkstone the road becomes a track. At the top go over a stile to fork left onto a track. After 200 yards cross a stile and go right on the well defined track. Before long the Hawick circuiar riding route comes in from the west and continues north with the Borders Abbeys Way for 400 yards before going off to the right. After the second hunt gate go down and a bit to right to a gateway. Go slightly left through young conifers to cross the Falla Cleugh Burn.

Climb up from the burn, keeping the dyke and fence to your right. The way is here a grass track but before long it drops to meet a more clearly defined track. After 800 yards go through a hunt gate and follow a path between a plantation and a wall until you enter a wood. The path is waymarked and leads through to a righthand turn down a track passing Salenside. Cross a bridge over the Ale Water and turn right onto a road just for 80 yards before going over a stile onto a track known as the Thief Road. Pass over a ladder-stile onto a golf course. Cross a bridge over a burn and cross over the golf course to turn left onto a track parallel with the fence. Pass through a series of gates and when the main track enters a wood leave it to go straight on to a second track. Turn right to reach a gateway and turn left onto the road just west of Wolrig.

Old ruined dovecot near The Haining, Selkirk

Carry along the road for just over a mile and just near the end of a section through a plantation notice on the right the Bishop's Stone, a large boulder set horizontally into the dyke probably to mark the boundary to the lands of the bishops of Glasgow in the parish of Ashkirk. Near here is the highest point of this section of the walk, at 1100ft. After another 400 yards turn right into a car park and pass through a wicket gate by the barrier. The forest road swings left and descends, giving a view of the Duke of Buccleugh's seat of Bowhill, a sprawling mansion mostly of several periods in the 19th century but with a nucleus of c1708. The road eventually drops down to cross the Middlestead Burn. When the road rises again turn off right uphill between trees for a short way. Turn right instead of following the riding route and go down between the fence and wood to pass through a wall at a junction of boundaries. Go up through trees, cross a stile over another wall and turn right onto a farm track to rejoin the riding route. Descend for 150 yards and pass through a gate to reach a double gate 400 yards further on. Keep on the track to another gate, with a wetland area on the right. The track then passes Middlestead farm steading to reach a road, where you turn right.

Scott's statue, Selkirk

Pass Brownmoor farm and go left over a stile opposite a small layby. Follow the edge of the field and turn left at a corner. Go right over a stile to reach a footbridge over the Hartwood Burn, then keep right over a stile along a field edge and over another stile to reach a farm track, following it left across a field after 800 yards. Continue on a grass track when the surfaced track ends. Pass left of a ruined mid 18th century dovecot to a stile onto a path through woods for a short distance. Turn right onto a track past the stables (now dwellings) added in 1819 to The Haining, Mark Pringle's mansion of 1794, which was damaged by a fire in 1944. Hidden beyond the house is a large overgrown mound upon which stood the castle of Selkirk, overlooking a small loch to the south. It was probably built by David, Earl of Huntingdon (later David I) during his brother Edgar's reign. Edward I of England had the palisades rebuilt in 1301-2, and a stone gatehouse was provided but they were destroyed by the Scots in 1313 and the site not used again. Go left onto the driveway of the house and pass under the arched gateway onto the road at West Port. From here go uphill to the right into the market square of Selkirk, which lies 57m from Melrose via Kelso and Jedburgh, and is 13m from Hawick.

Selkirk was made a royal burgh in the 1530s and had three gates and an earth rampart surmounted by a palisade. On the south side of Kirk Wynd is a graveyard containing a church of 1748 which was abandoned in 1863. Some graveslabs are older, and there was a church here in the 12th century, the original Kirk o' the Forest (of Ettrick) in which William Wallace is said to have been proclaimed Guardian of Scotland in 1297 after his victory at Stirling Bridge. At one time there was a medieval tower house in the High Street. Until the mid 18th century the town concentrated on making shoes, and later on textiles and linen were important, eventually leading to a trebling of the size of Selkirk to a population of about 6000. Numerous new mills opened beside the south side of Ettrick Water after a new road was built from Galashiels in 1833, whilst a branch railway arrived in the 1850s. Sir Walter Scott was sheriff here for the first third of the 19th century and the former town hall and sheriff courthouse of 1803-4 in the Market Place have been made into a museum celebrating his connection with Selkirk (see also page 23).

The Way continues up Kirk Wynd from Selkirk Market Place. Climb up to cross over the A7 and use the pavement on the left hand side of the A699. After passing a few houses turn left onto a waymarked path across common land to a kissing gate. Go right on to a track and pass through a hunt gate onto farmland. Go down a hawthorn lined track skirting the edge of Bell Hill and just before Greenhead Farm turn left through a hunt gate and follow the field edge to a seat with a view back over to Selkirk. Follow waymarks around the field edge to reach a road near Shawmount and turn right. Follow the road uphill heading east for two thirds of a mile and then go left through a white gate beside some stables. The woods here are called Halfcrown Corner, recalling the payment made by the Sunderland Estates to the men who planted the treees in the mid 19th century. Cross over a road onto a two mile section of old drove road which passes through several gates, keeping the dyke on your right. Go through a sheep-handling compound and then turn right to reach the the western tip of Cauldshiels Loch. Here Coot and Great Crested Grebe breed in the spring, and Tufted, Mallard and Goosander ducks use the loch in the winter. Birds such as the Redpoll, Bullfinch, Siskin and Long Tailed Tit use the willow and birch woodland for cover, and there are also Roe Deer here.

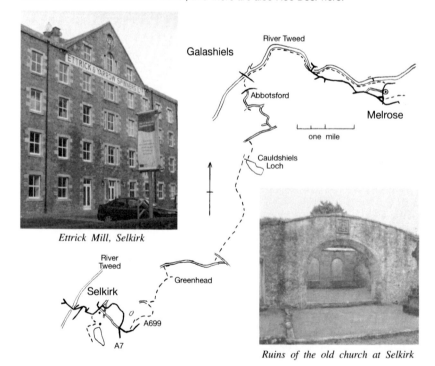

Ettrick Mill, Selkirk

Ruins of the old church at Selkirk

The main square of Selkirk

From the carpark near Cauldshiels Loch follow a track down through woods to turn right into a road. In half a mile turn left onto a winding lane past Abbotsmoss and then turn left on another lane which winds down to cross over the B6360, where there is a carpark. Here lies a house originally called Clarty Hole which Sir Walter Scott purchased and renamed Abbotsford. As Sheriff of Selkirk he was required to live in the county, and here he lived for the last twenty years prior to his death in 1832. The house is open to the public in the summer months and has a cafe near the entrance. Scott's collections still remain more or less as he left them. To start with Scott only had a modest house here but a new NE wing was added on the site of the original farmhouse after he was made a baronet by George IV in 1820, whilst the SW end now has rooms of the 1850s arranged around a small court. The walled garden to the SE contains bits of old sculptures.

Once over the B6360 a track curves round right to reach a ford across the Tweed which is used in June by the horse-riders of the Galashiels Common Riding. Turn right onto a track on the bank of the Tweed and go firstly under the viaduct of the A6091 and then after another half mile under the stone Redbridge Viaduct of the 1840s which carried the Edinburgh to Carlisle railway, which closed in 1969. The railway was known as the Waverley Route after one of Sir Walter Scott's novels. and this section of trackbed is now used by the Southern Upland Way to cross over the Tweed. Still on the riverbank, the Borders Abbeys Way passes Lowood House and goes through woodland. Turn left onto a drive and cross over a road. The final mile of riverside path leading along the north side of Melrose is shared with the Southern Upland Way, which eventually crosses the Tweed on a suspension bridge to head northwards. The Waverley Castle Hotel is built upon the site of a battle fought in 1526. Just beyond the suspension bridge turn right onto a road to come into the square of Melrose from the north, passing the abbey ruins. This completes a walk of 10 miles from Selkirk and a total of 67 miles if you have been round the full circuit via Kelso, Jedburgh and Hawick.

FURTHER READING

The Old Parish Churches of Scotland, Mike Salter, 1994.
The Castles of Lothian and the Borders, Mike Salter, 1994
Land's End to John O'Groats - A Thousand Mile Walking Route, Mike Salter 2006
The Southern Upland Way and St Cuthbert's Way, Mike Salter 2007
Borders - Buildings of Scotland series, Kitty Cruft, John Dunbar, Richard Fawcett, 2006
Royal Commission on Ancient and Historical Monuments inventories for the former
    counties of Roxburgh (1956) and Selkirk (1957). Other vols cover Peebles & Berwick
The Steel Bonnets (The Story of the Anglo-Scottish Reivers) G.Macdonald Fraser, 1964.
Guide pamphlets by Dept of Environment and Historic Scotland exist for the abbeys.

USEFUL WEBSITES AND OTHER INFORMATION

www.backpackersclub.co.uk - Club for those interested in backpacking in the UK.
www.campingandcaravanningclub.co.uk - Join to obtain details of extra camp sites.
www.geocaching.com   - Finding caches using a Global Positioning System (GPS).
www.ldwa.org.uk   - The Long Distance Walkers Association.
www.nationaltrail.co.uk   - Details of long-distance trails in UK.
www.syha.org.uk   - Scottish Youth Hostels Association.
www.traveline.org.uk   - Travel information throughout the UK
www.visitscotland.com   - Details of places to find accommodation in Scotland.

National Rail Enquiries: 08457 48 49 50.   For buses ring Traveline: 0870 608 2 608
Tourist Offices on or near the trail - Melrose, Kelso, Jedburgh, Hawick, Galashiels
The Backpackers Club provides members with information on places to pitch tents,
    both wild and on farmland with the owner's permission. It also arranges discounts
    on equipment from certain shops, and can suppy OS Maps at a much reduced price.
A Festival of Walking has been held in the Borders every year since 1995.

Entrance to Springfield Park, near Kelso